TAX STRATEGIES FOR THE ONE-PERSON BUSINESS
(2018-2019 Edition)

Written by
Christopher J. Inglese, CPA, MS (Tax)
Christopher J. Inglese, P.C.
703-847-8710
www.Scorporation.com

DISCLAIMER

This publication is designed to provide accurate and authoritative information in regard to the subject matter covered. It is sold with the understanding that the publisher is not engaged in rendering legal, accounting, or other professional service. If legal advice or other expert assistance is required, the services of a competent professional person should be sought.

Copyright © 2018 by Small Business Publishing, LLC

TABLE OF CONTENTS

OVERVIEW	3
UNDERSTANDING LEGAL ENTITIES VERSUS TAX TREATMENTS OF A ONE-PERSON BUSINESS	5
SAVING SELF-EMPLOYMENT TAX (FICA TAX)	9
MAXIMIZING THE 20% QUALIFIED BUSINESS INCOME DEDUCTION	15
SHIFTING INCOME TO LOW TAX BRACKET RELATIVES	19
DEFERRING TAX BY CONTRIBUTING UP TO 100% OF YOUR EARNED INCOME TO A RETIREMENT PLAN	23
DEDUCTING MEDICAL EXPENSES WITHOUT LIMITS	29
TAKING ADVANTAGE OF LOW TAX RATES ON CORPORATE INCOME AND ON DIVIDENDS	33
TAX STRATEGIES AVAILABLE ONLY TO CORPORATIONS	39
CONCLUSION	46
Appendix I – TAX-SAVING CHECKLIST	48
Appendix II – HOW JOE'S ONE-PERSON BUSINESS SAVES OVER $6,600 IN TAXES EACH YEAR	84

Copyright © 2018 by Small Business Publishing, LLC

OVERVIEW

Whether your business is organized as a corporation, a limited liability company, or a sole proprietorship, you (and/or your one-person business) are probably paying much more tax than is required by law, and don't even know it. Delegating all tax planning to your accountant, believing that he or she is providing you with the tax-saving advice you need, may be a big mistake.

Most accountants, who accept one-person businesses as clients, typically do not possess advanced tax education and/or in-depth tax experience. Many are too busy filling-in forms to provide innovative tax-saving advice to such small clients. Those who do in fact possess a Masters Degree in Taxation and have decades of professional experience, spend most of their time getting new business for their firm and managing their staff. It is the low-level staff person who is assigned to the one-person business, while knowledgeable and experienced tax accountants focus their tax planning skills on larger businesses and wealthier individuals.

This booklet is intended to explain, in plain English, the most valuable and widely applicable tax-saving strategies available to the one-person business. It is up to you to familiarize yourself with these strategies, and then consult with your present tax advisor to determine if they

Copyright © 2018 by Small Business Publishing, LLC

are appropriate in your particular situation. <u>You are ultimately responsible for the taxes you pay.</u>

The majority of one-person businesses unfortunately pay thousands of dollars in unnecessary taxes each year. Don't be one of them.

Copyright © 2018 by Small Business Publishing, LLC

UNDERSTANDING LEGAL ENTITIES VERSUS TAX TREATMENTS OF A ONE-PERSON BUSINESS

A one-person business can operate under one of three different legal forms:

- Sole Proprietorship
- Limited Liability Company
- Corporation

A limited liability company (LLC) with one owner, which does not elect to be treated as a corporation, is treated as a sole proprietor for tax purposes. A corporation or LLC can elect to be taxed as an S corporation, or in the absence of an S election, could be considered either a personal service corporation or a regular corporation. The legal form of the business therefore does not necessarily control these four different tax treatments available to the one-person business:

SOLE PROPRIETORSHIP or DISREGARDED LLC ENTITY

As mentioned above, absent an election, a one-person limited liability company is disregarded as an entity. Income from such businesses is reported each calendar year on Schedule C of the owner's individual income tax

Copyright © 2018 by Small Business Publishing, LLC

Form 1040 and is taxed at the owner's personal tax rates. All of the business income is considered "earned" by the owner, and is subject to self-employment tax (also known as FICA, which is comprised of Social Security tax and Medicare tax). The owner is required to remit taxes via estimated tax payments each "tax quarter".

Subject to certain limitations, sole proprietors may be entitled to a Qualified Business Income Deduction (explained later) equal to 20% of their net profit.

S CORPORATION

A corporation or LLC, which makes an "Election by a Small Business Corporation" using IRS Form 2553, is generally not considered a tax-paying entity. Net income from the S corporation (after deducting the shareholder-employee's salary and bonus) is reported each calendar (or fiscal) year on Schedule E of the shareholder-employee's individual income tax Form 1040 and is generally subject to only income tax at the owner's personal tax rates. (There is no additional tax at the time the S corporation distributes currently or previously taxed profits.)

Salary and/or bonus payments to the shareholder-employee are the only amounts considered "earned" by him/her and therefore only these amounts are subject to FICA taxes (as well as income tax). The shareholder-employee's FICA and income taxes are withheld from his/her salary and bonus. (Estimated tax payments might also be required to cover taxes on income reported on Schedule E.)

Subject to certain limitations, shareholders of S corporations may be entitled to a Qualified Business Income Deduction (explained later) equal to 20% of their net income from the S corporation, after deducting the shareholder-employee's salary and bonus.

PERSONAL SERVICE CORPORATION

A one-person corporation, or an LLC which has elected to be taxed as such, which is engaged in one of the professions (health, law, engineering, architecture, accounting, actuarial science, the performing arts, or consulting) is considered a personal service corporation. Net income from such a corporation (after deducting the shareholder-employee's salary and bonus) is taxable to the corporation at the flat federal tax rate of 21%. This same income (not paid out to the shareholder- employee as salary or bonus) is generally taxed again when distributed to the shareholder. Because it is often difficult for a personal service corporation to justify retaining income for non-tax reasons, all income is typically paid out as salary and bonus to the shareholder-employee in order to avoid an accumulated earnings tax and double taxation. The salary and bonus is considered "earned" by the shareholder-employee and therefore subject to FICA taxes (as well as income tax). The shareholder-employee's FICA and income taxes are withheld from his/her salary and bonus.

As a result of tax law changes under the Tax Cuts and Jobs Act, there are less differences between the tax treatments of personal service corporations and regular corporations after 2017.

REGULAR CORPORATION

Net income (after deducting the shareholder-employee's salary and bonus) from a corporation, or an LLC which has elected to be taxed as such, which is neither an S corporation nor a personal service corporation, is taxable to the corporation at a flat 21% federal tax rate. This same income (the amount not paid out to the shareholder-employee as salary or bonus) is generally taxed again when distributed to the shareholder. (To avoid this double taxation, a regular corporation may pay out some or all of its income each year as salary and bonus to the shareholder-employee.) The salary and bonus is considered "earned" by the shareholder-employee and therefore subject to FICA taxes (as well as income tax). The shareholder-employee's FICA and income taxes are withheld from his/her salary and bonus. (Corporate estimated tax payments might also be required to cover taxes on the income that is taxable to the corporation.)

Copyright © 2018 by Small Business Publishing, LLC

SAVING SELF-EMPLOYMENT TAX (FICA TAX)

GENERAL TAX STRATEGY

Self-employment tax (also known as FICA tax) is comprised of Social Security and Medicare taxes. It is generally imposed only on a taxpayer's "earned income". The typical American taxpayer pays more in self-employment tax and/or FICA tax than he/she does in income tax. The general tax strategy is to clearly separate "earned income" from "unearned income", so that the self-employment tax (or FICA tax) is imposed only on income earned from the labor or services provided by the taxpayer. Even though saving the Social Security portion of the FICA tax now, may result in a reduction in future government benefits later, it is generally believed that the taxes saved can be better invested by the taxpayer to yield a much greater future retirement benefit.

SOLE PROPRIETORSHIP OR DISREGARDED LLC ENTITY

Since all income reported on Schedule C of Form 1040 is subject to self-employment tax, there is little a sole proprietor (or owner of a disregarded limited liability company) can do to save self-employment tax. However, he or she can hire his/her children under the age of

Copyright © 2018 by Small Business Publishing, LLC

eighteen and the "reasonable" wages paid to such children are not subject to FICA tax, but still reduce the parent-owner's self-employment tax. (See the section entitled SHIFTING INCOME TO LOW BRACKET FAMILY MEMBERS regarding additional potential income tax savings.) Also, self-employment tax can be saved by properly allocating portions of deductible expenses to Schedule C (ex/ business portion of income tax preparation fee, portion of car loan interest and property tax relating to its business use, etc).

S CORPORATION

Since only the shareholder-employee's salary and bonus are subject to payroll tax, S corporations provide an opportunity to separate "earned income" from "unearned income", thereby saving a significant amount of FICA tax. By reducing the shareholder-employee's salary and bonus ("earned income") to a low but "reasonable" level, only that amount of income will be subject to FICA tax. The remaining non-salary income, not subject to FICA tax, can be withdrawn tax-free as a distribution of profits.

It is unclear what comprises a "reasonable" level of salary and bonus. Court cases and IRS rulings have confirmed that $0 is not "reasonable" compensation. Some of the factors to consider when determining a shareholder-employee's "reasonable" salary and bonus are:

- the time spent working by the shareholder-employee
- the type of work being performed by the shareholder-employee
- the salaries of non-shareholder-employees doing similar work
- the portion of profits derived from labor of non-shareholder-employees
- the portion of profits derived from capital invested in the corporation

The Social Security portion of the FICA tax rate is 12.4% of wages up to $128,400 (in 2018), while the Medicare portion of the FICA tax rate is 2.9% of all wages. There is however an additional .9% employee Obamacare tax on wages in excess of $125,000 (if Married Filing Separate), $200,000 (if Single) or $250,000 (if Married Filing Joint). The 12.4% and 2.9% rates are paid 50/50 by the employer and the employee, with the employer's half deductible for income tax purposes. Since a shareholder in a one-person business is both the employer and the employee, the actual FICA tax rate for someone in the 22% income tax bracket would be about 13.62% on the first $128,400 (in 2018). If a shareholder-employee were to reduce his salary and bonus from $85,000 to $60,000, about $3,405 in after-tax FICA could be saved every tax year. However, if the shareholder-employee has wages from outside the S corporation, that when combined with S corporation wages exceed the annual $128,400 Social Security wage base, then higher Social Security tax would be incurred

Copyright © 2018 by Small Business Publishing, LLC

as a result of incorporation (or electing to be taxed as a corporation).

If an unmarried sole proprietor, with $200,000 of Schedule C income, were to incorporate and set his/her salary at $128,400, approximately $1,848 of Medicare tax could be saved every tax year (after taking into account a 22% employer income tax deduction). The savings could even be higher if such sole proprietor's Schedule C income is in excess of $200,000 (by avoiding the additional .9% Medicare tax).

It is important to note that a 3.8% Obamacare tax is also imposed on "unearned income" for taxpayers with Adjusted Gross Incomes in excess of $125,000 (if Married Filing Separate), $200,000 (if Single) or $250,000 (if Married Filing Joint). The profit from an S corporation, that flows through to shareholders who "materially participate" in the business, is not considered "unearned income". This Obamacare tax will therefore generally not be imposed on net income from one-person S corporations.

PERSONAL SERVICE CORPORATION

A personal service corporation's net income (after deducting the shareholder-employee's salary and bonus) is taxable to the corporation at the flat rate of 21%. Whatever income is left, after the payment of this

Copyright © 2018 by Small Business Publishing, LLC

corporate-level tax, is generally taxed again to the shareholder when distributed. Since personal service corporations are not capital-intensive businesses, it may be difficult for them to avoid the possible imposition of an accumulated earnings tax. For this reason, it is typically beneficial to zero-out the income taxable to the corporation by maximizing the shareholder-employee's salary and bonus before each year-end. However, by paying out all income to the shareholder-employee in this way, all of the business income becomes subject to FICA tax. As a result, the shareholder-employee of a personal service corporation can do little to reduce FICA tax.

REGULAR CORPORATION

Like an S corporation, a regular corporation must pay a "reasonable" salary to its shareholder-employees. A regular corporation's net income (after deducting the shareholder-employee's salary and bonus) is taxable to the corporation at a flat 21% tax rate, then it is typically taxed again to the shareholder when distributed. If the shareholder is in a very high marginal tax bracket, it may be beneficial to reduce the shareholder-employee's salary and bonus each year so that some earnings are retained by, and thus taxable to, the corporation. The goal is to ensure that the net income left in the corporation is taxed at a marginal income tax rate that is measurably lower than the shareholder-employee's marginal income tax rate. In addition to this income tax savings, limiting the salary and bonus paid to the shareholder-employee also avoids FICA tax. There is also no FICA tax when the net income, which was left in the corporation, is eventually distributed to the shareholder as a dividend. (See later section entitled TAKING ADVANTAGE OF LOW TAX RATES ON CORPORATE INCOME AND ON DIVIDENDS for a more detailed discussion of this topic.)

MAXIMIZING THE 20% QUALIFIED BUSINESS INCOME TAX DEDUCTION

GENERAL TAX RULES

Under the Tax Cuts and Jobs Act, effective January 1, 2018, individuals who own an interest in a qualified domestic business are generally entitled to take an income tax deduction equal to 20% of the lower of the net income from such business or their taxable income (after subtracting any net long-term capital gains).

However business owners, whose personal overall taxable income (before the 20% deduction) exceeds $415,000 (married filing joint) or $207,500 (others), are not allowed to take the 20% deduction if their business is considered a "specified service business". Such a business is one that performs services in the fields of consulting, health, law, accounting, actuarial science, performing arts, athletics, financial services, brokerage services, or any trade or any business where the principal asset is reputation or skill of one or more of its employees or owners. This limitation is phased-in for married taxpayers filing jointly whose taxable income is between $315,000 and $415,000, or other taxpayers

Copyright © 2018 by Small Business Publishing, LLC

whose taxable income is between $157,500 and $207,500.

In addition, these same higher income business owners are also subject to a wage limitation. That is, the 20% deduction generally cannot exceed the greater of
- 50% of the compensation paid to employees, or
- 25% of the compensation paid to employees, plus 2.5% of the undepreciated basis of tangible property

Like the limitation on "specified service businesses", this limitation is also phased-in for married taxpayers filing jointly whose taxable income is between $315,000 and $415,000, or other taxpayers whose taxable income is between $157,500 and $207,500.

SOLE PROPRIETORSHIP or DISREGARDED LLC ENTITY

Since a sole proprietor or owner of a single member disregarded LLC does not take a salary/bonus from the business, the 20% Qualified Business Income Deduction is based on the entire profit (reported on Schedule C).

One-person business owners, with taxable income below the $315,000 / $157,500 thresholds, will need to weigh the income tax savings from a proprietorship's larger Qualified Business Income Deduction (computed without any reduction for owner's salary/bonus) against the additional self-employment tax cost that the sole proprietor pays (and S corporation owner avoids on the profit remaining after paying "reasonable compensation"), adjusted for any reduction in the owner's future Social Security benefits.

One-person business owners, with taxable income above the $315,000 / $157,500 thresholds, would get no (or little) Qualified Business Income Deduction if the business either has no employees or is a "specified service business".

S CORPORATION

The 20% Qualified Business Income Deduction is based only on net income from an S corporation, after deducting the shareholder-employee's salary/bonus.

One-person business owners, with taxable income below the $315,000 / $157,500 thresholds, will need to weigh the self-employment tax savings from an S corporation against the income tax cost of having a smaller Qualified Business Income Deduction and any reduction in the owner's future Social Security benefits (as compared to a sole proprietor).

One-person businesses who have high taxable income may want to consider S corporation status, where they are considered employees and must be paid a "reasonable compensation" amount. Assuming the business is not a "specified service business" (previously defined), such compensation might allow the owner to take an otherwise unallowable 20% Qualified Business Income Deduction.

PERSONAL SERVICE CORPORATION

Personal service corporations are not entitled to take the Qualified Business Income Deduction.

REGULAR CORPORATION

Regular corporations are not entitled to take the Qualified Business Income Deduction.

SHIFTING INCOME TO LOW BRACKET RELATIVES

GENERAL TAX STRATEGY

Each individual taxpayer pays income tax based on a graduated tax rate schedule, with marginal federal income tax rates ranging from 0% to 37%. Individuals with higher income therefore pay tax at higher marginal rates. The general tax strategy is to save income tax by "shifting" income from taxpayers subject to the higher tax rates (ex/ 37%), to taxpayers subject to the lower rates (ex/ 0%). Of course, no one wants to "shift" their income to an unrelated person just to avoid tax. (No one wants to give up $1.00 to save only $.37.) However, one might consider saving tax by "shifting" income to a low tax bracket relative who will benefit from that income anyway, such as a dependent child or parent.

SOLE PROPRIETORSHIP OR DISREGARDED LLC ENTITY

Since all income of a sole proprietorship, or disregarded limited liability company, is reported on Schedule C of Form 1040, such a taxpayer can "shift" income by hiring his/her relative (typically a child or parent). As long as a "reasonable" salary or wage is paid to the relative, the taxpayer can save tax by deducting it as a business expense. The low tax bracket relative, reporting the salary or wage as income on his/her own individual tax return, pays little or no income tax.

The taxpayer should be able to prove "reasonableness", by having the relative keep timesheets detailing the work he/she does each day. Since salary or wage income is considered "earned income", it is not subject to the tax rule which taxes "unearned income" of children under the age of 19 (and some full-time students age 19 to 23) at higher marginal tax rates. See above section entitled SAVING SELF-EMPLOYMENT TAX (aka FICA) regarding additional potential self-employment tax savings of hiring children under the age of eighteen.

S CORPORATION

Since income from an S corporation is reported each year on the individual income tax returns of its shareholders, based on their percentage of stock ownership, S corporations provide a unique opportunity to "shift" income by issuing stock to low tax bracket relatives. A child or parent, owning 25% of the S corporation's stock, will report 25% of the income from the S corporation on his/her personal tax return. In order for this tax strategy to work, it is important that the child or parent be the "true" owner of the stock, not just the "legal" owner. He or she must behave as a shareholder and exercise his/her power as such. It is also important that "reasonable" wages be paid to all shareholder-employees for services actually performed. Lastly, shareholder children must be at least 24 years of age (18 if not a student or if child's earned income exceeds his/her support), if corporate income is to be taxed at their low individual tax rates, rather than the higher rates prescribed by law.

Unlike a sole proprietorship or disregarded limited liability company, FICA tax is incurred if an S corporation pays salaries or wages to children of shareholder-employees (regardless of their age). However, since there is no FICA tax on S corporation profits (after deducting the shareholder-employees' "reasonable" salaries and bonuses), there is a FICA tax advantage to shifting income via the issuance of S corporation stock (rather than via the payment of salaries and wages) to low tax bracket relatives.

PERSONAL SERVICE CORPORATION

Like a sole proprietorship, or disregarded limited liability company, a personal service corporation usually "shifts" income only by employing its shareholder-employee's relative (typically a child or parent) at a "reasonable" salary or wage. This is the case since it is often beneficial to zero-out the income taxable to a personal service corporation, primarily through the use of salaries and bonuses, before each year-end.

Copyright © 2018 by Small Business Publishing, LLC

REGULAR CORPORATION

Net income retained in a regular corporation (after deducting salaries and wages of its shareholder-employees) is generally taxed first at the corporate level, then again at the shareholder level when that income is distributed as dividends. Because dividends must be paid in proportion to stock ownership, and low tax bracket relatives typically are minority shareholders, it is generally better to "shift" income via the payment of salaries and wages, rather than the issuance of regular corporate stock. However, issuing stock to low tax bracket relatives, and paying dividends to them, may make sense where all of the shareholder-employees are in low tax rate brackets (12% or less on salary and wage income, and 0% on dividend income).

When determining the amount of salaries and wages to be paid to relatives, the overriding goal is to ensure that salaries and wages are "reasonable", and that the net income left in the corporation is taxed at a marginal income tax rate that is lower than that of the shareholder-employee. (See later section entitled TAKING ADVANTAGE OF LOW TAX RATES ON CORPORATE INCOME AND ON DIVIDENDS for a more detailed discussion of this topic.)

Copyright © 2018 by Small Business Publishing, LLC

DEFERRING TAX BY CONTRIBUTING UP TO 100% OF YOUR EARNED INCOME TO A RETIREMENT PLAN

GENERAL TAX STRATEGY

Like a Traditional IRA, money contributed to a retirement plan is deductible and its earnings grow tax-deferred. Income tax is incurred only when the original contribution and its earnings are distributed, typically when the individual taxpayer is retired (and usually in a low tax bracket). The tax deduction for the contribution allows the taxpayer to earn income on money that otherwise would have been paid in income tax. The tax-deferred earnings compound each year, allowing the money to grow faster (without the imposition of income tax). The general tax strategy is therefore to maximize contributions to retirement plans (to the extent allowed by law).

There are many types of retirement plans available to the one-person business (such as the SEP, the SIMPLE-IRA, the 401(k) Profit Sharing Plan, and the Defined Benefit Plan). This booklet will focus on only the 401(k) Profit Sharing Plan which, other than perhaps the Defined

Copyright © 2018 by Small Business Publishing, LLC

Benefit Plan, allows the maximum contribution for the one-person business. A SIMPLE-IRA (which is similar to the 401(k) Profit Sharing Plan) should be considered by the smaller one-person business with limited funds.

The amount that can be contributed to a 401(k) Profit Sharing Plan is comprised of an employee contribution plus an employer contribution. The maximum employee contribution for the 2018 tax year is $18,500 ($24,500 for an employee age 50 and older). In 2018, the maximum employer contribution rate is 25% (on up to $275,000 of "earned income"). The total of both these amounts cannot exceed an overall maximum amount of $55,000 in 2018 ($61,000 if age 50 and older). The 401(k) Profit Sharing Plan (as well as the SIMPLE-IRA) allows up to 100% of "earned income" to be contributed to the retirement plan. In 2018, a one-person business, with earned income of $24,667, can contribute all $24,667 to the retirement plan (25% of $24,667, plus $18,500 from the employee-owner assuming he/she is less than 50 years of age).

The 401(k) Profit Sharing Plan is fairly flexible. The employee need not make a contribution. The employer typically must make "substantial and recurring" contributions, though not every year. (For "safe harbor" plans, the employer contributions may have to equal 3% to 4% of "earned income".) The Plan need not cover part-time employees (those working under 1,000 hours a year), nor employees under age 21 (ex/ children of the owner). The 401(k) Profit Sharing Plan should be in existence for at least 4 to 6 years, or the life of the business (whichever is shorter).

As long as the owner and/or his/her spouse are the only employees, there is very little administration. When total retirement plan balances reach $250,000 or more, the fairly simple 5500EZ form must then be filed (within 7 months of the business year-end). It is important to note that if employees (other than the owner's spouse or children under age 21) are hired, the costs of administering a 401(k) Profit Sharing Plan could be approximately $1,000 or more per year. In this case, a SIMPLE-IRA should be considered, in lieu of the 401(k) Profit Sharing Plan, to avoid the administration costs.

It is important to note that retirement plan contributions lower both adjusted gross income and taxable income, thus potentially increasing the allowable portion of certain deductions (such as the Qualified Business Income Deduction).

SOLE PROPRIETORSHIP OR DISREGARDED LLC ENTITY

All income reported by a sole proprietorship or disregarded limited liability company is considered "earned" income. As a result, this type of one-person business, with a "safe harbor" 401(k) Profit Sharing Plan, is required to make an employer contribution equal to 3% to 4% of the Schedule C income (adjusted for the contribution itself, as well as the deduction for one-half of the self-employment tax). As a result of this complex calculation, the owner has little control over the amount of the minimum required contribution each year. Also, since a sole proprietorship or disregarded limited liability company pays more self-employment tax than other types of one-person businesses, the maximum allowable Profit Sharing contribution is lower (because of the higher subtraction adjustment for one-half of this additional self-employment tax).

S CORPORATION

Since only the shareholder-employee's salary and bonus is considered "earned income", an S corporation with a "safe harbor" 401(k) Profit Sharing Plan, would be required to make an employer contribution equal to 3% to 4% of only that salary and bonus. As a result, by adjusting his salary and bonus each year, the shareholder-employee has a great deal of control over the amount of the annual minimum contribution required each year.

In order to reach a combined employee and employer contribution of $55,000 (2018 maximum), a shareholder-employee under the age of 50 must have a salary and bonus totaling only $146,000 ($55,000 equals the employer contribution of 25% of $146,000, plus the

$18,500 employee contribution). Sole proprietorships or disregarded limited liability companies, must have higher "earned income" in order to reach the same $55,000 maximum. In addition, the owner of these other non-corporate entities pay extra self-employment tax on any earnings in excess of the amount needed to reach the maximum 401(k) contribution. The S corporation thus may allow its shareholder-employee to optimize his/her salary and bonus, to maximize the 401(k) Profit Sharing contributions while minimizing the FICA taxes.

PERSONAL SERVICE CORPORATION

It is typically beneficial to zero-out the income taxable to a personal service corporation through the use of salaries and bonuses (as well as related FICA tax and retirement plan contribution deductions) before each year-end. As a result, this type of corporation has little control over the amount of its 3% to 4% minimum required 401(k) "safe harbor" contribution each year. Also, the personal service corporation and its shareholder-employee might pay extra FICA taxes on salaries, in excess of the amount needed to reach the maximum 401(k) contribution.

REGULAR CORPORATION

The overriding goal in a regular corporation is to ensure that the net income left in the corporation (after the deductions for salaries, bonuses, employer FICA tax, and retirement plan contributions) is taxed at a marginal income tax rate that is significantly lower than that of the shareholder-employee. Tax deductions for employer FICA tax expense and employer retirement plan contributions, must be considered in reaching this goal.

DEDUCTING MEDICAL EXPENSES WITHOUT LIMITS

GENERAL TAX STRATEGY

Medical expenses and health insurance of an individual, and his/her dependents, are generally deductible on Schedule A of Form 1040, but only to the extent they are in excess of 7.5% of his/her Adjusted Gross Income. For this reason, most individuals get little or no income tax deduction for medical expenses and health insurance paid from personal after-tax funds. The general tax strategy is therefore to arrange to have the one-person business pay such health-related expenses and deduct them as a business expense (a fringe benefit to its employee).

In the past, any business could have set up a non-discriminatory Medical Expense Reimbursement Plan (MERP), or Health Reimbursement Arrangement (HRA), to reimburse employees' (and/or their family's) medical expenses and personal health insurance policy premiums. The business deducted such reimbursements as an employee fringe benefit business expense, saving the owner both income tax and self-employment tax. Only the owner-employees had to report the reimbursement of medical expense or health insurance premiums as income.

However, under The Affordable Care Act (aka Obamacare), any such plan or arrangement (other than a qualified Small Business HRA) that covers two or more employees is now illegal, with the business owner subject to a $100 per day per employee penalty for not complying with the "government-approved" scheme.

SOLE PROPRIETORSHIP OR DISREGARDED LLC ENTITY

There is a "tax loophole", available to the sole proprietorship or disregarded limited liability company, when the owner's spouse is the only legitimate employee of the business. Since there is only one employee, Obamacare does not apply and the company can offer an otherwise unallowable employee fringe benefit. It may set up a plan to reimburse and deduct medical expenses and premiums relating to a family health insurance policy in the name of the proprietor's employee-spouse. Such plan covers not just the employee, but also his/her own spouse and dependents. In other words, all medical-related expenses of the owner and his/her family are tax deductible, by virtue of the fact that the owner is the spouse of the covered employee.

The Medical Reimbursement Plan, or Health Reimbursement Arrangement, must be written and established before the reimbursable medical expenses are incurred.

Copyright © 2018 by Small Business Publishing, LLC

S CORPORATION

There is no income tax deduction allowed for most fringe benefits (example/ Medical Expense Reimbursement Plan), provided by S corporations to shareholders who own greater than 2% of its stock. Fringe benefits provided to family members of such shareholders are also generally not deductible, regardless if those family members are employees of the S corporation. Under IRS Notice 2008-1 (which pre-dates Obamacare), the shareholder-employee, and any family member employees, must report health insurance premium reimbursements received as W-2 income. However, if qualified, such employees may be entitled to the "above-the-line" Self-employed Health Insurance Deduction. (The IRS is contemplating whether S corporations, that reimburse personal health insurance premiums for only shareholder-employees, or employees related to shareholder-employees, are subject to the $100 per day per employee penalty.)

PERSONAL SERVICE CORPORATION

A shareholder, who is the sole employee of a personal service corporation, may have such corporation reimburse his medical expenses and personal health insurance premiums without having to report the expense reimbursement as personal income. The corporation deducts such reimbursements, as an employee fringe benefit business expense, without limitation.

The Medical Expense Reimbursement Plan, or Health Reimbursement Arrangement, must be written and established before the reimbursable medical expenses are incurred.

REGULAR CORPORATION

A shareholder, who is the sole employee of a personal service corporation, may have such corporation reimburse his medical expenses and personal health insurance premiums without having to report the expense reimbursement as personal income. The corporation deducts such reimbursements, as an employee fringe benefit business expense, without limitation.

The Medical Expense Reimbursement Plan, or Health Reimbursement Arrangement, must be written and established before the reimbursable medical expenses are incurred.

TAKING ADVANTAGE OF LOW TAX RATES ON CORPORATE INCOME AND ON DIVIDENDS

GENERAL TAX STRATEGY

Regular corporate income, not paid to a shareholder-employee as salary or bonus, is taxed at the flat corporate federal tax rate of 21%. When this income is distributed to the shareholder, it is taxed as a dividend typically at the 15% tax rate (0% if the taxpayer is in the 10% or 12% income tax brackets, and 20% if the taxpayer is in the higher tax brackets). The general tax strategy is to minimize taxes by properly setting the shareholder-employee's salary and bonus to "split" income between the corporation and that shareholder-employee, taking advantage of the lowest possible tax rates of each (considering FICA taxes as well). The individual-level income tax can also be deferred by delaying the taxable dividend (or capital gain) to the shareholder until a future year.

SOLE PROPRIETORSHIP OR DISREGARDED LLC ENTITY

Because a sole proprietorship and a disregarded limited liability company are not considered taxpayers separate

Copyright © 2018 by Small Business Publishing, LLC

from their owner, these entities cannot take advantage of low tax rates on corporate income and dividends.

S CORPORATION

Income and/or deductions of an S corporation are reported on the income tax return of its owner. The highest corporate tax rate may be imposed on any income that, in special circumstances, is taxed simultaneously at both the individual owner and corporate levels. For this reason, the S corporation cannot split income to take advantage of low tax rates on corporate income and dividends.

PERSONAL SERVICE CORPORATION

Like a regular corporation, net income of a personal service corporation (after deducting the shareholder-employee's salary and bonus) is taxable to the corporation at the flat corporate tax rate of 21%. A shareholder of such a corporation tends to live off of the business profits and the business is more likely subject to an accumulated earnings tax. For these reasons, most (if not all) of a personal service corporation's net income is typically paid out each year as salary and bonus to its shareholder-employee. However, for a personal service corporation that has a non-tax reason to justify a lower salary to its shareholder-employee and retain earnings, there may be a tax benefit by taking advantage of the low tax rates on corporate income and dividends. (See the following discussion concerning regular corporations.)

REGULAR CORPORATION

INCOME TAX RATES

Regular corporations are considered separate taxpayers, subject to a flat federal income tax rate of 21%. The corporate net income (the amount that is not paid out to the shareholder-employee as salary or bonus) is generally taxed again at the 15% federal rate when distributed to the shareholder (0% if the shareholder is in the 10% or 12% personal marginal tax bracket). Higher income taxpayers are subject to a 20% rate.

FICA TAX RATES

The Social Security portion of the FICA tax rate is 12.4% of wages up to the "Social Security wage base" ($128,400 in 2018). The Medicare portion of the FICA tax rate is 2.9% of all wages, plus an additional .9% Obamacare tax on wages in excess of $125,000, $200,000 or $250,000 (depending on filing status). The 12.4% and 2.9% rates are paid 50/50 by the employer and by the employee, with the employer's half deductible for income tax purposes. Since a shareholder in a one-person business is both the employer and employee, the actual combined employer and employee FICA tax rate would be at least 13.69% on wages up to the "Social Security wage base" and 2.60% on wages over that base amount (after adjusting for the corporate-employer's tax savings at the 21% federal income tax bracket). If the shareholder-employee has wages from other sources equal to or greater than the "Social Security wage base", the actual combined FICA tax rate would be at least 7.49% on wages up to the Social Security wage base.

DIVIDENDS PAID
Taxes might be saved if the shareholder-employee's "reasonable" salary is set to keep him/her in the 22% (or lower) federal income tax bracket. Assume this is done, with the corporation itself reporting $50,000 of taxable income, and the $39,500 ($50,000 - (21% x $50,000)) of after-tax funds being paid to the shareholder-employee as a dividend (rather than as a bonus). In this case, ignoring state income taxes, the corporation would pay $10,500 of income tax (21% of $50,000) and the shareholder-employee would pay $5,925 of income tax on the dividend (15% x ($50,000 - $10,500)). The total combined federal tax paid by the corporation ($10,500) and the shareholder-employee ($5,925) would be $16,425 (or 32.85% of $50,000).

BONUS PAID
However, if the $50,000 were paid out by the corporation, via a $46,447 bonus to the shareholder-employee and $3,553 of employer FICA tax (7.65% of $46,447), then the corporation would pay the $3,553 in employer FICA tax (no income tax). If the shareholder-

employee is subject to both the Social Security and Medicare taxes (his/her total wages from all sources total less than the "Social Security wage base" of $128,400 in 2018), but not the additional .9% Obamacare tax, then he/she would then pay $3,553 in employee FICA tax (7.65% of $46,447) and $10,218 in income tax (22% of $46,447), for a total individual federal tax bill of $13,771. The total combined federal tax paid by the corporation ($3,553) and the shareholder-employee ($13,771) would be $17,325 (or 34.65% of $50,000).

TAX SAVINGS
In this example, approximately $900 (1.80% of $50,000) might be saved if the salary of a shareholder-employee were set, so that the corporation itself reported $50,000 of taxable income, with the $39,500 of after-tax corporate funds paid to the shareholder-employee as a dividend (rather than as a bonus).

If the taxpayer were in an income tax bracket higher than 22% and/or subject to the .9% Obamacare tax, then the tax savings would be even greater. Even if the taxpayer were in the lower 10% or 12% tax brackets, he/she would still enjoy tax savings by being able to take advantage of a 0% tax rate on dividend income. Also, if the taxable dividend of $39,500 were paid to the shareholder (or included as part of a capital gain on the sale or liquidation of the business) in a future year, the $5,925 income tax (15% of $39,500) would be deferred, and compound interest could be earned each year on this $5,925. If there was a non-tax business reason for not ever paying the dividend, or the shareholder never sold or liquidated the business, then the $5,925 tax could be entirely avoided upon the shareholder's death.

However note that if a taxpayer is in the 24% or lower income tax bracket and has total "reasonable" salaries from all sources greater than the "Social Security wage base", then paying the shareholder a dividend, rather than a bonus, might result in a higher overall tax liability (since such bonus would only subject the shareholder-employee to Medicare tax and not to Social Security tax).

Also note that the above analysis ignores the impact of state income taxes imposed on both the corporation and individual, as well as the loss of future Social Security benefits, when income is received as a dividend (rather than as salary or bonus subject to Social Security tax).

Copyright © 2018 by Small Business Publishing, LLC

TAX STRATEGIES AVAILABLE ONLY TO CORPORATIONS

WITHHOLDING STRATEGY

Penalties may be imposed if the owner of a one-person business fails to pay his/her taxes throughout the tax year. Taxes withheld from salary or bonus payments are considered as paid evenly throughout the tax year, regardless of when the salary or bonus is actually paid. There is no penalty imposed if income tax withholding (or evenly paid estimated tax payments) equals or exceeds a "safe harbor" of 100% of the "total tax" reported on the owner's prior year personal tax return (110% if prior year Adjusted Gross Income was over $150,000).

Based on the above rules, the general tax strategy is to withhold from salary and bonus payments of shareholder-employees, income taxes equal to the "safe harbor" percentage of his/her previous year's "total tax" liability. The goal is to avoid the requirement for filing personal estimated tax vouchers, while not incurring penalties for the underpayment of tax throughout the year. By paying taxes through the withholding process, the actual payment of tax can occur very late in the tax year (when the salary or bonus is paid), rather than evenly throughout the tax year (when individual estimated tax

Copyright © 2018 by Small Business Publishing, LLC

payments are required). This improves the cash flow of the business and allows interest to be earned during the tax year on the deferred tax.

A shareholder-employee's optimal salary and bonus is determined each year, depending on the type of corporation, marginal income tax brackets, FICA taxes, and desired retirement plan contributions. If the optimal salary and bonus is not large enough to cover both the employee FICA tax and "safe harbor" withholding, then it may be advisable to make quarterly individual estimated tax payments, rather than increase the salary or bonus (since an increase in salary or bonus may result in additional FICA and income taxes, which might be greater than the penalty that could be avoided).

FISCAL YEAR-END STRATEGY

Corporations are allowed to have any fiscal year-end other than and including December 31st. Personal service corporations and S corporations typically must make an election under Section 444 of the Internal Revenue Code to have a fiscal year-end (no earlier than September 30th) in their initial tax year.

A shareholder reports S corporation income on his/her personal income tax return in the calendar year in which the S corporation's fiscal year ends. If the S corporation has a fiscal year-end of September 30, 2018, then the

Copyright © 2018 by Small Business Publishing, LLC

shareholder reports only income from October 1, 2017 through September 30, 2018 on his/her personal 2018 income tax return. The S corporation must however remit a refundable deposit to the IRS, intended to approximate the income tax on deferred earnings from the end of the fiscal year until December 31st. The calculation of the deposit works roughly (though not exactly) like this:

If an S corporation reported income (before deducting salary and bonus to its shareholder-employee) of $120,000 for the 12 month period ended September 30, 2018, it is "deemed" to have made $30,000 for the three-month period from October 1, 2018 through December 31, 2018. A tax rate equal to 1% above the highest individual tax rate (38.00% in 2018) is applied to the $30,000, less any salary or bonus paid to the shareholder-employee from October 1, 2017 through December 31, 2017, to arrive at the required deposit due May 15, 2018.

Each year the refundable deposit is adjusted, using the S corporation's profit (or loss) for the prior tax period.

A fiscal year-end might be beneficial to an S corporation owner in the following situations:

- The business is seasonal and actual income from October 1 through December 31 is more than the calculated "deemed" income (ex/ retailer with a busy Christmas season).

Copyright © 2018 by Small Business Publishing, LLC

- The business is growing and actual income from October 1 through December 31 is more than the calculated "deemed" income (based on the prior twelve month period, which may have included lower income and start-up expenses).
- The shareholder-employee is in a high individual tax bracket and the business is located in a state with no fiscal year-end deposit requirement.

In these cases, the required refundable deposit may be less than the combined federal and state income taxes that would be due if the S corporation did not have a fiscal year-end.

It may also be beneficial for the S corporation shareholder to know the business income to be reported on his/her personal tax return before December 31st. If the shareholder determines that he/she will be in a higher tax bracket next year, a bonus could be paid from the S corporation immediately before December 31st. The bonus will appear as W-2 income in the current year and will be taxed at the lower current year rate. The bonus will reduce the net K-1 income to be reported by the shareholder next year, when he/she is in a higher tax bracket. This strategy benefits businesses that are cyclical in nature, where income is higher one year, but lower the next (ex/ a political consultant who makes money primarily during the federal elections that are held every other year).

Copyright © 2018 by Small Business Publishing, LLC

It is important to note that a fiscal year-end can be elected only during the beginning months of the S corporation's initial year. Once an S corporation has a December 31 year-end it generally may not change to a fiscal year-end. An S corporation with a fiscal year-end may however switch to a calendar year-end by having its shareholder pay tax on more than 12 months of income on his/her Form 1040. In this case, the balance of the federal fiscal year-end deposit is refunded (typically after the due date of the Form 1040).

Personal service corporations generally must pay salary and/or bonus to shareholder-employees before December 31st, equal to the income earned from October 1 through December 31st. If this is not done, the corporation may lose some of its deduction for the salary and/or bonus. There is little tax benefit for a personal service corporation to have a fiscal year-end.

Regular corporations may have a fiscal year-end as early as January 31st. In this case, if the bulk of a shareholder-employee's salary and/or bonus could be paid in January with little or no withholding, then the corporation could basically get a tax deduction for salary and/or bonus almost one year before the shareholder-employee would have to report the same as income.

SOCIAL SECURITY BENEFIT STRATEGY

Early Social Security benefits (taken by individuals before reaching full retirement age) are reduced for those recipients who have "earned income" above a certain threshold each year. "Unearned income" however may be received by these individuals without limit and without any reduction of their Social Security benefits. "Unearned income" includes rents, interest and dividends from corporations. Keeping the salary and bonus paid to a shareholder-employee at a low, but reasonable, level (while distributing corporate profits via dividends) may preserve Social Security benefits.

EXCLUSION FOR GAIN FROM SMALL BUSINESS STOCK

Individuals who own stock in certain small business corporations for more than five years, may exclude from taxation a percentage of the gain from the sale of such stock (100% for stock acquired after 9/27/10). Generally, the stock must be newly issued by a regular corporation with at least 80% of its assets used in the active conduct of a qualified trade or business (which excludes professional services, consulting, hospitality, finance, insurance, farming and mining).

FRINGE BENEFIT STRATEGY

Personal service corporations and regular corporations are able to deduct certain fringe benefits without requiring the shareholder-employee, and/or his/her employee-relative, to report such benefits as income. Fringe benefits include accident and health plans (including long-term care insurance), group-term life insurance, dependent care assistance, disability insurance, educational assistance, qualified transportation benefits, retirement advice, contributions to "education savings accounts", cafeteria plans, qualified employee discounts, no additional cost services, working condition fringes, on-premises athletic facilities, and "de minimis" fringes. S corporations, sole proprietorships, and limited liability companies are able to provide only some of these benefits to its shareholder-employee on a tax-advantaged basis. Each fringe benefit is subject to various qualifications and reporting requirements, the discussion of which is beyond the scope of this book.

Copyright © 2018 by Small Business Publishing, LLC

CONCLUSION

If you are a sole proprietor (or disregarded limited liability company) you may want to form a corporation (or elect to have your limited liability company treated as such). If you are a corporation, you may want to adjust your salary and bonus (and/or your present or future dividends) and related tax withholdings. If you work alone, you may want to hire your spouse, children, or dependent relatives. If you have a SEP, but wish you could make more tax-deductible contributions, you might want to set up a 401(k) Profit Sharing Plan instead. If you and/or your family have significant medical expenses, you might want to consider establishing a Medical Expense Reimbursement Plan.

This booklet is intended to educate and inform you, the one-person business owner. It offers creative and valuable suggestions on how your overall taxes might be reduced. By reading the ideas contained in this book and using the following checklist, you will be able to discuss your taxes intelligently with your tax advisor, and determine if he or she is capable of giving you the proper advice. Only after thorough discussions with a qualified and competent tax professional, should you consider any of the tax-saving ideas presented as being appropriate for you or your business.

Copyright © 2018 by Small Business Publishing, LLC

With proper tax planning, a significant amount of taxes may be saved each and every year. It is well worth your effort.

Copyright © 2018 by Small Business Publishing, LLC

TAX-SAVING CHECKLIST FOR THE ONE-PERSON BUSINESS

Question	Comment

<u>Registering the Business</u>

If a corporation, or the business has employees:

    Have you obtained a "Federal Employer Identification Number" (Form SS-4)? _____

    Have you obtained a state tax number? _____

    Have you obtained an unemployment tax Number (if different than the state tax number)? _____

Have you received a business license and/or occupancy permit from the county or city in which business is conducted? _____

If the business has more than two employees, has it purchased worker's compensation insurance? _____

If the business is "doing business" in more than one state, has it registered with the other state's tax department and/or secretary of state? _____

Copyright © 2018 by Small Business Publishing, LLC

TAX-SAVING CHECKLIST FOR THE ONE-PERSON BUSINESS

Question	Comment
If a corporation, or if the business has employees, is owner aware of the responsibility to collect and/or pay:	
- federal corporate income tax?	_____
- federal withholding and FICA taxes?	_____
- federal unemployment tax?	_____
- state corporate income tax?	_____
- state withholding tax?	_____
- state unemployment tax?	_____
- state corporate fee?	_____
Is the business aware of the responsibility to collect and/or pay:	
- state use tax?	_____
- state sales tax?	_____
- county business license tax?	_____
- county personal property tax?	_____
- other tax (ex/ litter, tire, etc)?	_____

Copyright © 2018 by Small Business Publishing, LLC

TAX-SAVING CHECKLIST FOR THE ONE-PERSON BUSINESS

Question	Comment
Deciding whether to be an S Corp (rather than a C Corp)	
Is your business eligible to make an S election:	
- a domestic LLC or corp.?	_____
- under 100 equity owners?	_____
- only one class of stock?	_____
- all owners are individuals, estates, or qualified trusts?	_____
- not a certain type of bank, DISC or insurance company?	_____
Will your business have no trouble remaining eligible for S status?	_____
Is your taxable income low enough, or your business not a "specified service business", and therefore eligible to take the 20% Qualified Business Income Deduction?	_____
Does your business expect to distribute to you, rather than reinvest, most of its earnings?	_____
Is there a good chance that your business will either be liquidated or sold in the near future?	_____

Copyright © 2018 by Small Business Publishing, LLC

TAX-SAVING CHECKLIST FOR THE ONE-PERSON BUSINESS

Question	Comment
Does your business expect to have start-up losses which you could use to reduce your own personal taxes?	_____
Can you be reasonably compensated at a salary level somewhat below the Social Security wage base?	_____
Is the FICA Tax savings (from electing S status and taking compensation below business profit) more than the income tax savings (from the lower 21% tax rate on corporate-level income and 0% - 20% rate on shareholders' dividend income) and reduction in future Social Security benefits?	_____
Will your business have only marginal benefit from having a fiscal year-end other than September, October, November, or December?	_____
Do the states, in which your corporation or LLC does business, recognize the federal S election?	_____
Upon IRS audit, is it possible that business tax deductions could be disallowed and reclassified as dividend distributions?	_____

Copyright © 2018 by Small Business Publishing, LLC

TAX-SAVING CHECKLIST FOR THE ONE-PERSON BUSINESS

Question	Comment
Are the costs of statutory fringe benefits (ex/ group life, medical & disability plans) provided to you, the owner-employee, insignificant?	_____
Does your business contemplate no (or little) investment in dividend-paying stock of other corporations?	_____
Could the your personal taxes be reduced by issuing stock (thereby shifting income or loss) to your family members?	_____
Do you incur interest expense, relating to your investment in the business, which is not currently deductible (due to your lack of investment income)?	_____
Would your business be unable to utilize the cash method of accounting (ex/ its average revenue exceeds $25 million) if it were not an S corporation?	_____

Copyright © 2018 by Small Business Publishing, LLC

TAX-SAVING CHECKLIST FOR THE ONE-PERSON BUSINESS

Question	Comment
Could your business be subject to the Personal Holding Company or Accumulated Earnings Tax if it were not an S corporation?	_____
Will your corporation be newly-formed (or your LLC elect corporate status) and therefore have no built-in gains or C corporation attributes or carryovers?	_____
Is your business in a field that would preclude you from excluding up to 100% of the gain from the sale of qualified small business stock in a regular corporation?	_____

Copyright © 2018 by Small Business Publishing, LLC

TAX-SAVING CHECKLIST FOR THE ONE-PERSON BUSINESS

Question	Comment

Deciding whether to be taxed as a Proprietor (rather than an S Corp)

Is your "reasonable" compensation equal to, or only a bit less than the net business profit? _____

Is the Self-Employment Tax savings (from electing S status and taking compensation below the net profit of your business) less than the additional income tax savings (from having a larger 20% Qualified Business Income Deduction) and higher future Social Security benefits? _____

Do you <u>not</u> need to be considered an employee of your business and paid a salary or wage, in order to qualify for the 20% Qualified Business Income Deduction? _____

Will your business have no benefit from a September, October, November, or December year-end? _____

Do the states, in which your corporation or LLC does business, not recognize S elections? _____

Would there be no or little personal tax savings if your business income was distributed to your family members and taxed at their marginal tax rates? _____

Copyright © 2018 by Small Business Publishing, LLC

TAX-SAVING CHECKLIST FOR THE ONE-PERSON BUSINESS

Question	Comment
Do you incur interest expense, or property taxes, relating to the business use of your personal car, which is not currently deductible?	_____
Do you prefer to pay estimated income tax payments each "quarter", rather than paying once a year through the withholding process?	_____
Does your business employ your children who are under the age of 18?	_____
If you are receiving early Social Security benefits, is your business income less than the allowable amount above which such benefits are reduced?	_____
If you have a home office, are you worried that upon audit the IRS might reclassify your business occupancy cost reimbursements as "rent" (jeopardizing their deductibility)?	_____
Does the cost of preparing corporate income tax returns and payroll tax returns outweigh the benefits of being taxed as an S corporation?	_____
Does the business have losses or distributions that are being financed by the business entity's debt that you have personally guaranteed?	_____

Copyright © 2018 by Small Business Publishing, LLC

TAX-SAVING CHECKLIST FOR THE ONE-PERSON BUSINESS

Do you have wages from a job that, when combined with the net profit of your business, exceeds the Social Security wage base ($128,400 in 2018)? _____

Does your spouse work in your business and does your family have significant medical expenses not covered by your current health insurance? _____

Copyright © 2018 by Small Business Publishing, LLC

TAX-SAVING CHECKLIST FOR THE ONE-PERSON BUSINESS

Question	Comment
Deciding Ownership and Issuing Stock	
If an S corporation, might stock be issued to your low-income children (at least 18, or in some cases 24, years of age), or parents, to take advantage of their lower tax bracket?	_____
If an S corporation, might interest expense, incurred on debt used to either acquire or carry the stock, be fully deductible on Schedule E of personal return?	_____
If a C corporation, might interest expense, you incurred on debt use to either acquire or carry your stock, be deductible (to the extent of investment income) on Form 4952 of your own return?	_____
If a corporation, in deciding which assets to contribute in exchange for its stock, has the exclusion of property with either a mortgage over its tax basis or an unrealized loss, been considered?	_____

Copyright © 2018 by Small Business Publishing, LLC

TAX-SAVING CHECKLIST FOR THE ONE-PERSON BUSINESS

Question	Comment
If a corporation, would an ordinary deduction (rather than capital loss) be available in the event the corporate stock were sold at a loss or were to become worthless:	
- common stock issued by domestic corp?	_____
- stock issued in exchange for money or property (other than securities)?	_____
- total assets received by the corporation for its stock < $1 million?	_____
- less than 50% of corporation's receipts (past 5 yrs) from passive sources?	_____
- the loss treated as ordinary is $50,000 ($100,000 if joint) per year?	_____
If an LLC, is either the husband or wife members (but not both), in order to avoid the imposition of self-employment tax on two people (rather than one)?	_____

Copyright © 2018 by Small Business Publishing, LLC

TAX-SAVING CHECKLIST FOR THE ONE-PERSON BUSINESS

Question	Comment

Borrowing Funds

If a disregarded LLC or sole proprietor, have you separated debt used for business from other debt (ex/ business credit card, business use portion of car loan, etc), and deducted the interest related to business expenditures on Schedule C? _____

If an S corporation, have you capitalized the business by borrowing money personally (rather than guaranteeing corporate debt); thus ensuring a current deduction of losses, or avoiding a taxable distribution (financed by borrowed funds) on your personal tax returns? _____

If a C corporation, have you at least partially capitalized the business by loaning money to your corporation (rather than contributing capital) thus enabling you to receive repayment in the future without tax consequences? _____

If a corporation, are your loans to/from the corporation properly documented with written notes which, if greater than $10K in aggregate, bear reasonable interest? _____

Copyright © 2018 by Small Business Publishing, LLC

TAX-SAVING CHECKLIST FOR THE ONE-PERSON BUSINESS

Question	Comment
If a corporation, have you avoided the necessity to pay non-deductible interest on funds borrowed from the corporation to finance your personal expenditures (unless such borrowings qualify as home acquisition or equity indebtedness)?	_____
Might the business borrow funds from your children (at least 18, or in some cases 24, years old) who are in a low tax bracket so as to reduce your family's overall income taxes?	_____
If an S corporation, are you aware that you may recognize income when your loans to the corporation (which have previously financed corporate losses deducted on your personal income tax returns) are repaid?	_____

Copyright © 2018 by Small Business Publishing, LLC

TAX-SAVING CHECKLIST FOR THE ONE-PERSON BUSINESS

Question	Comment
Acquiring Furniture & Equipment	
Are depreciation write-offs being maximized through the timing of property acquisitions and the careful use of the IRC Section 179 expensing election?	_____
Has an inventory of all the property being used by the business been taken (to include assets purchased in prior years for personal use and now use for business) to increase depreciation deductions or decrease property taxes?	_____
If a corporation, will the corporation purchase the depreciating assets it will use in its business (rather than having you purchase and lease them to the corporation) to avoid having you incur non-deductible passive activity losses?	_____
If a corporation, will you personally purchase the appreciating assets (ex/ real estate) the corporation will use, thus avoiding the recognition of corporate level taxable income when the assets are either distributed to you (S corp) or disposed of (C corp)?	_____

Copyright © 2018 by Small Business Publishing, LLC

TAX-SAVING CHECKLIST FOR THE ONE-PERSON BUSINESS

Question	Comment
Has the business adopted a set standard to differentiate repairs and supplies (currently deductible) from capital expenditures (depreciable over time)?	_____
Is the business making the annual tax De Minimis Safe Harbor Election under IRS Reg 1.263(a)-1(f) allowing the write-off each year of individual items of property costing $2,500 or less?	_____
If the business owns a building, is the annual Safe Harbor Election for Small Taxpayers under IRS Reg 1.263(a)-3(h) being made each year, allowing for the write-off of repairs, maintenance, etc?	_____
Does the business review its property acquisitions each year to segregate "personal property" purchases (rapidly deducted) from "real property" purchases (slowly depreciated)?	_____
Has the availability of "bonus depreciation" been considered to accelerate the deduction for the purchase of new property (that has not been expensed under IRC Section 179 mentioned above)?	_____

Copyright © 2018 by Small Business Publishing, LLC

TAX-SAVING CHECKLIST FOR THE ONE-PERSON BUSINESS

Question	Comment
Selecting Accounting Period and Methods	
If a PSC or an S corporation, has a Section 444 election (to have a year-end other than December 31st) been considered to possibly defer taxes and improve your personal tax planning?	_____
If a C corporation (not a PSC), has a fiscal year been considered so that the personal income taxes on your year-end bonus can be deferred to the next year?	_____
Is your business electing to use the accrual method of accounting only when it sells inventory, its payables are expected to rise faster than its receivables, or the cash method is otherwise prohibited by law?	_____
If the business, with gross receipts under $25 million, is engaged in the performance of long-term contracts, has the completed-contract method of accounting been considered as a possible method to defer income tax?	_____

Copyright © 2018 by Small Business Publishing, LLC

TAX-SAVING CHECKLIST FOR THE ONE-PERSON BUSINESS

Question	Comment
If the business is engaged in the sale of inventory, has it considered the simplified LIFO method of accounting to defer tax when inventory levels and costs are rising?	_____
Is the business, with gross receipts over $25 million, aware of the interest and uniform capitalization rules for constructed property and inventory?	_____
Has the use of the installment sale method of reporting gain on the disposition of non-dealer property been considered to defer taxes into a lower bracket year and to increase interest earnings for the corporation?	_____
If a C corporation, and part of an affiliated group, has a consolidated income tax return been considered?	_____

Copyright © 2018 by Small Business Publishing, LLC

TAX-SAVING CHECKLIST FOR THE ONE-PERSON BUSINESS

Question	Comment

Compensating Shareholder-Employees

If taxed as an S corporation, might overall payroll and income taxes be saved by paying you the lowest reasonable salary and distributing excess earnings as dividends? _____

If a C corporation, does the corporation pay you the proper amount of "reasonable" compensation and year-end bonus each year (to take advantage of both corporate and graduated personal tax rate schedules)? _____

Have you considered withholding from your (or your spouse's) salary or year-end bonus, those income taxes sufficient to avoid underpayment penalties and/or the necessity for estimated tax filings? _____

If you are being compensated by two or more related corporations, have you considered using a common paymaster to avoid paying unnecessary payroll taxes? _____

Copyright © 2018 by Small Business Publishing, LLC

TAX-SAVING CHECKLIST FOR THE ONE-PERSON BUSINESS

Question	Comment
If you are receiving early Social Security benefits, have you considered having your business taxed as a corporation, and paying yourself a low but reasonable salary, in order to preserve full payment of those benefits by avoiding the earned income limitations?	_____
If an S corporation, have you considered reducing your salary if it is presently causing an S corporation loss which cannot be deducted on your personal tax return?	_____
If a C corporation, would you be able to rebuff an IRS challenge as to the reasonableness of your compensation and thereby avoid having the compensation recast as non-deductible dividends (which would be double taxed)?	_____
If a C corporation, is your compensation documented in the corporation's minutes, to make it more difficult for the IRS to reclassify it to a non-deductible dividend distribution?	_____

Copyright © 2018 by Small Business Publishing, LLC

TAX-SAVING CHECKLIST FOR THE ONE-PERSON BUSINESS

Question	Comment
Hiring Family and Outside Contractors	
Is the business reducing its employment tax costs by hiring legitimate "independent contractors" who cannot be considered disguised "employees" by IRS (Form SS-8)?	_____
Is the business maintaining proper records for new employees (W-4 & I-9) and independent contractors (W-9)?	_____
Does the business send 1099-MISC forms to its non-corporate independent contractors, lawyers, and landlords who are paid at least $600 each year for personal services they perform?	_____
Has the business considered hiring your spouse on a full or part-time basis and paying him/her a low (but reasonable) wage in order to: - Cover him/her under the business retirement plan (ex/ 401(k)plan)	_____
- Provide other fringe benefits to him/her (ex/ "medical expense reimbursement plan")	_____

Copyright © 2018 by Small Business Publishing, LLC

TAX-SAVING CHECKLIST FOR THE ONE-PERSON BUSINESS

Question	Comment
- take the child care credit and/or deduct spousal travel, business meals, entertainment, and education?	
Has the business considered hiring your children (or parents) who have very little or no other income and paying them an amount equal to their standard deduction (plus perhaps an IRA deduction) in order to:	
- Save income taxes?	
- Save self-employment taxes (if a disregarded LLC or sole proprietor, hires a child under the age of 18)?	
Have you considered taking your children (or parents) off the business's payroll (personally giving them gifts instead) to save FICA and income tax (when they are in a higher tax bracket than you)?	
If your parents have small estates (below the exemption) and are in a low income tax bracket, have you considered giving them some ownership in your corporation or having the business pay them wages which (along with gifts from you) they could use to purchase a home or other appreciating asset (which then could be willed to you tax-free)?	

Copyright © 2018 by Small Business Publishing, LLC

TAX-SAVING CHECKLIST FOR THE ONE-PERSON BUSINESS

Question	Comment

Providing Benefits to Employees

If a C corporation, have the following fringe benefit programs (which can be provided to you and other employees on a tax-free basis) been considered:
- group term life insurance (to $50K)? _____
- medical expense reimbursement plan (HRA)? _____
- health and hospitalization plans? _____
- disability income plans? _____
- meals & lodging furnished for the convenience of the employer? _____
- cafeteria plans? _____

If a corporation, does the business reimburse you for business expenses you incur on a "dollar for dollar" basis (rather than through an expense allowance) in order to avoid unnecessary payroll taxes and to minimize your income taxes? _____

If an S corporation sponsors, or pays for, a health insurance plan which covers you and/or family members, have your premiums been included in your W-2 taxable wages, excluded from Social Security withholding (assuming no discrimination in health coverage) and deducted (to the extent allowable by law) on your personal income tax returns? _____

Copyright © 2018 by Small Business Publishing, LLC

TAX-SAVING CHECKLIST FOR THE ONE-PERSON BUSINESS

Question	Comment
If a disregarded LLC or sole proprietor, has the business considered hiring your spouse and setting up a "medical expense reimbursement plan", which reimburses (and deducts) medical expenses for your spouse and his/her family (which includes you and your children)?	_____
Have you or the business considered setting-up a Health Savings Account program?	_____
If a corporation, has the business considered contributing to your child's Education Savings Account, or paying for retirement planning services?	_____
If a disregarded LLC or sole proprietor, has the business considered setting up a "Small Business Health Reimbursement Arrangement", which reimburses (and deducts) medical expenses for your employees (which may include you and your family)?	_____

Copyright © 2018 by Small Business Publishing, LLC

TAX-SAVING CHECKLIST FOR THE ONE-PERSON BUSINESS

Question	Comment

Leasing Assets

Do you analyze whether it is better for the business to lease or buy furniture and equipment by computing after-tax present values under each alternative?   _____

Have personal property leases been reviewed in order to determine whether each is a regular (operating) or capital (finance) lease so that proper tax deductions (ex/ Section 179 expense deduction) can be computed? _____

Is it possible to shift taxable income to your child (at least 18, or in some cases 24, years of age) who is in a low tax bracket by having the business lease assets from him/her? _____

If your business has signed an office lease calling for either a period of free rent, or for escalating rents, has the presence of an imputed rent expense deduction been investigated? _____

Copyright © 2018 by Small Business Publishing, LLC

TAX-SAVING CHECKLIST FOR THE ONE-PERSON BUSINESS

Question	Comment
Have you considered having your corporation construct improvements on land, that it is leasing from you, which will revert to you at the end of the lease term, possibly without tax?	
If your business is involved in leasing an automobile, has the "income inclusion" amount been properly reported on the income tax return?	
If your business's principal place of business is located in your home, is it possible to take a deduction based on the IRS allowance of $5 per square foot (up to 300 square feet), OR for the business use portion of the actual utilities, repairs, maintenance, and depreciation of the home (based on the square footage used for business and documented by photographs and an occupancy permit)?	
If a corporation, can occupancy expenses be reimbursed rather than having your corporation "rent" the office space from you?	

Copyright © 2018 by Small Business Publishing, LLC

TAX-SAVING CHECKLIST FOR THE ONE-PERSON BUSINESS

Question	Comment

Using a Car for Business

Have you prepared an analysis to determine if it is better for your corporation (rather than you) to own a business vehicle, deduct the related interest, treat the vehicle as if it were used 100% for business, and include an amount of income in your W-2 for the value of your personal usage? _____

Are vehicle-related deductions being maximized through a comparison of the actual cost method with the standard mileage method, in the year the vehicle is first used for business? _____

Is written evidence relating to business vs. personal vehicle use being maintained as insurance against an IRS adjustment? _____

If the standard mileage method to compute vehicle deductions is being used, are the business use portion of car loan interest and personal property taxes also being deducted, and records of the vehicle's basis being maintained? _____

Copyright © 2018 by Small Business Publishing, LLC

TAX-SAVING CHECKLIST FOR THE ONE-PERSON BUSINESS

Question	Comment
Is the minimum amount of a "luxury" automobile's cost being expensed (under Section 179) so that the current year's maximum write-off is unaffected but the depreciation deductions in the years immediately following the purchase of the automobile are increased?	_____
Do you plan the business use of your vehicle to exceed 50%, thus allowing the Section 179 expense and accelerated depreciation deductions?	_____
Have you considered buying an SUV on the last day of your tax year and using it 100% for business that day, in order to get a Section 179 deduction equal to 100% of its cost? (Note that future business use must be > 50% to avoid "recapture" of the deduction.)	_____

Copyright © 2018 by Small Business Publishing, LLC

TAX-SAVING CHECKLIST FOR THE ONE-PERSON BUSINESS

Question	Comment

Entertaining, Traveling and Giving Gifts

Are you maintaining adequate records for business travel, and meals (which include date, place, dollar amount, persons present, business relationships and the topic of "substantial business discussions")? _____

Does your business account for deductible business meals separately from non-deductible business entertainment? _____

Has the business considered having its clients/customers reimburse it for actual meal and entertainment expenditures thus avoiding the 50% reduction by having the reduction passed on to those clients/customers? _____

Are business gifts deducted only up to $25 per donee per year and are records documenting the business relationships of the donees maintained? _____

TAX-SAVING CHECKLIST FOR THE ONE-PERSON BUSINESS

Question	Comment
With respect to out-of-town business travel, are you deducting transportation costs to and from the destination by having "business days" (over four hours spent on business) exceed "pleasure" days?	_____
Are you deducting the dry cleaning and laundering expenses for clothes soiled while you were away on a business trip (regardless of where the dry cleaning is done)?	_____
Have you considered deducting the standard IRS per diem for travel meals and incidental expenses, rather than actual costs?	_____

Copyright © 2018 by Small Business Publishing, LLC

TAX-SAVING CHECKLIST FOR THE ONE-PERSON BUSINESS

Question	Comment
Distributing Earnings	
If a C corporation, are you analyzing whether to pay out earnings to yourself in the form of compensation (deductible by the corporation, but subject to FICA), or in the form of dividends (which are non-deductible by the corporation and therefore taxed twice)?	_____
If an S corporation, have you determined how best to structure the transfer of funds to you from the corporation (dividend distribution, loan, salary, fringe benefits, expense reimbursement)?	_____
If an S corporation, even with relatives as shareholders, are dividend distributions paid in proportion to stock ownership to avoid inadvertently terminating the S election?	_____
If an S corporation, are dividend distributions documented in the corporation's minutes, to make it more difficult for the IRS to reclassify them to FICA taxable compensation?	_____

Copyright © 2018 by Small Business Publishing, LLC

TAX-SAVING CHECKLIST FOR THE ONE-PERSON BUSINESS

Question	Comment
If an S corporation, are distributions taken only to the extent of your basis in the corporation (your investment plus your share of cumulative undistributed corporate earnings) in order to avoid a taxable gain?	_____
If an S corporation, have you considered exchanging the debt owed to you by the corporation (the basis of which has been reduced by your share of corporate losses) for additional shares of stock, in order to avoid a taxable loan repayment or distribution, and improve the borrowing power of the corporation?	_____

Copyright © 2018 by Small Business Publishing, LLC

TAX-SAVING CHECKLIST FOR THE ONE-PERSON BUSINESS

Question	Comment

Planning for Retirement

Have you considered setting up a retirement plan in order to defer tax on your share of business earnings and to compensate family-employees on a tax-deferred basis? _____

Have you considered terminating (or merging) an existing Money Purchase Pension Plan, in light of the increased contribution limits for Profit Sharing Plans and Simplified Employee Pensions? _____

Before adopting a Simplified Employee Pension, have the following factors been considered:
- maximum of 25% of compensation can be contributed (up to $55,000 in 2018)? _____
- no requirement to make contributions? _____
- both full-time employees & part-time workers (who have worked 3 of past 5 years earning $600/year (in 2018) must be eligible to participate? _____
- immediate 100% vesting of all contributions is required? _____
- investments selected by employee? _____
- easy & inexpensive administration (no annual government filings)? _____

Copyright © 2018 by Small Business Publishing, LLC

TAX-SAVING CHECKLIST FOR THE ONE-PERSON BUSINESS

Question	Comment
Before adopting a Profit Sharing Plan, have the following factors been considered:	
- maximum of 25% of compensation can be contributed (up to $55,000 in 2018)?	_____
- contribution amounts may vary but must be "recurring and substantial"?	_____
- only full-time employees over 21 with 1 year of service (2 years if plan calls for immediate vesting) must be eligible to participate?	_____
- up to 6 years may be required for 100% vesting?	_____
- investments selected by either corporate employer or employee?	_____
- administration is fairly simple and inexpensive (annual 5500EZ required if > $250,000 in one-person plan)?	_____
Before adopting a Defined Benefit Pension Plan, have the following factors been considered:	
- maximum contribution is the amount which, when deposited on behalf of an employee each year until he/she retires, will yield an annual benefit of no more than the lesser of his/her highest 3 consecutive years of compensation, or $220,000 (2018 limit) for the remainder of the employee's life?	_____

Copyright © 2018 by Small Business Publishing, LLC

TAX-SAVING CHECKLIST FOR THE ONE-PERSON BUSINESS

Question	Comment
- contributions are required each year?	_____
- only full-time employees over 21 with 1 year of service (2 years if plan calls for immediate vesting) must be eligible to participate?	_____
- up to 6 years may be required for 100% vesting?	_____
- investments selected by either corporate employer or employee?	_____
- administration is very complex and expensive requiring the use of an actuary (annual government filing are required each year)?	_____
If the business has set up a retirement plan, has it considered providing tax-free "qualified retirement planning services" to you?	_____
Before adopting a Savings Incentive Match Plan for Employees (SIMPLE), have the following factors been considered: - maximum annual contribution of $12,500 (2018 limit) by each employee under age 50, or $15,500 (2018 limit) by each employee over age 50?	_____

Copyright © 2018 by Small Business Publishing, LLC

TAX-SAVING CHECKLIST FOR THE ONE-PERSON BUSINESS

Question	Comment
- employer must generally either match employee contributions up to 3% of employee's compensation; or else make a 2% of compensation contribution on behalf of each eligible employee?	_____
- employees who received a least $5,000 in compensation from the employer the two previous years, and are expected to receive that amount during the year, are eligible for the plan?	_____
- immediate 100% vesting is required?	_____
- investments selected by either corporate employer of employee?	_____
- administration is fairly simple and inexpensive (annual government filing is required only by trustee)?	_____

Before adopting a "one-person" 401(k) Profit Sharing Plan (husband and wife considered "one person") have the following factors been considered:

- the 2018 maximum annual contribution of $18,500 by each employee under age 50 ($24,500 by each employee 50 or over)?	_____
- the employee elective deferrals are not taken into account in applying the above profit sharing deduction limits to the corporate employee contributions?	_____

Copyright © 2018 by Small Business Publishing, LLC

TAX-SAVING CHECKLIST FOR THE ONE-PERSON BUSINESS

Question	Comment
Has the advice of a qualified pension consultant been obtained?	_____

HOW JOE's ONE-PERSON BUSINESS SAVES OVER $6,600 IN TAXES EACH YEAR

SCENARIO

Joe, age 49, is a consultant who works on his own. He is married and has a 20 year old daughter. Joe's 45 year old wife works part-time as his office manager, but is not paid for her work. His daughter also helps out in the summers without pay. She has no income.

Joe's business is organized as an LLC (treated as a sole proprietorship) with its income and deductions reported on Schedule C of his personal individual tax form 1040. The business grosses $180,000 and nets $120,000 (after paying expenses to vendors). Out of the $120,000, Joe contributes the maximum Simplified Employee Pension (SEP-IRA) plan contribution of $22,304 (($120,000 – ($120,000 x .9235 x 15.3% x ½)) x 20%) each year. In Joe's last job, he was paid a salary of $60,000 per year for doing the same basic work he now performs in his own business. Joe and his wife are in the 22% marginal tax bracket and expect to be in the 12% tax bracket when they retire. They live in a state without income tax.

Based on his historical Social Security earnings record, Joe is only in the 15% marginal income replacement tier (for computing Social Security retirement benefits).

The next two pages explain how Joe uses his one-person business to save over $6,000 in taxes each year.

Copyright © 2018 by Small Business Publishing, LLC

ELECTING TO BE TAXED AS AN S CORPORATION

Rather than having his business treated as a sole proprietorship, Joe files Form 2553 (Election by a Small Business Corporation), to have the LLC business treated as an S corporation. He has the S corporation LLC pay him a "reasonable" salary of $60,000. As a result, Joe and his business now pays net Social Security and Medicare taxes of about $8,170 (($60,000 x 15.3%)-(22% x ½ x $60,000 x 15.3%)), rather than paying net self-employment tax of about $15,090 (($120,000 x 92.35% x 15.3%)-(22% x ½ x $120,000 x 92.35% x 15.3%)). **Joe saves about $6,920 of self-employment tax each year** (that he can invest for a return that will more than compensate for his lower Social Security benefits).

HIRING DAUGHTER

Rather than having his daughter work in the summer without pay, Joe has the S corporation LLC pay her $3,000 for the summer. As a result, Joe (via the S corporation) and his daughter will incur gross Social Security and Medicare taxes of about $459 ($3,000 x 15.3%). However, since his daughter's income is below her standard deduction, Joe will save about $710 in income tax (($3,000 x 22%) + ($3,000 x 15.3% x ½ x 22%)). **Joe saves about $251 of net tax each year.**

SETTING UP A 401(k) PROFIT SHARING PLAN

Rather than contributing only $16,728 to a SEP-IRA, Joe has the S corporation LLC establish a 401(k) plan in which he can make a

$18,500 contribution as an "employee" (based on 2018 maximum) as well as the S corporation LLC making a $15,000 contribution as an "employer" (25% x $60,000). As a result, Joe can deduct an additional $11,196 (($18,500 + $15,000) - $22,304) of retirement plan contributions and save about $2,463 in current income tax (22% x $11,196).

Rather than having his wife work without pay, Joe has the S corporation LLC pay her $24,667 per year. As a result, Joe (via the S corporation) and his wife will incur net Social Security and Medicare taxes of about $3,359 (($24,667 x 15.3%) – (22% x ½ x $24,667 x 15.3%)), but be able to deduct $24,667 of additional retirement plan contributions. The $24,667, which is comprised of an $18,500 contribution by the wife as an "employee" plus a $6,167 contribution by the S corporation LLC (25% x $24,667), immediately saves about $5,427 in income tax (22% x $24,667).

Together Joe and his wife can contribute an additional $35,863 ($11,196 + $24,667) to the retirement plan. Though taxable in the future when distributed from the plan, earnings on retirement plan assets grow tax-deferred, and **the contributions save Joe and his wife about $4,531 in current taxes each year** ($2,463 + $5,427 - $3,359).

LOSS OF 20% QUALIFIED BUSINESS INCOME DEDUCTION

As a result of the above, the 20% Qualified Business Income deduction has been reduced from $24,000 (20% x $120,000) down to only $892 (20% x ($120,000 - $60,000 PAYROLL - $4,590 ER FICA - $15,000 ER PS - $3,000 PAYROLL - $230 ER EFICA - $24,667 PAYROLL - $1,887 ER FICA - $6,167 ER PS)), resulting in **an income tax increase of $5,084** (22% x ($24,000 - $892)).

Copyright © 2018 by Small Business Publishing, LLC

CONCLUSION

By simply –

(1) Electing to be taxed as an S corporation (to avoid self-employment tax),

(2) Hiring his daughter (to shift income to a low tax bracket relative), and

(3) Setting up a 401(k) Profit Sharing Plan and hiring his wife (to defer tax by contributing up to 100% of her salary to a retirement plan)

Joe saves about $6,618 of <u>net</u> taxes each year.

How much are you saving?

Copyright © 2018 by Small Business Publishing, LLC

Made in the USA
San Bernardino, CA
01 June 2019